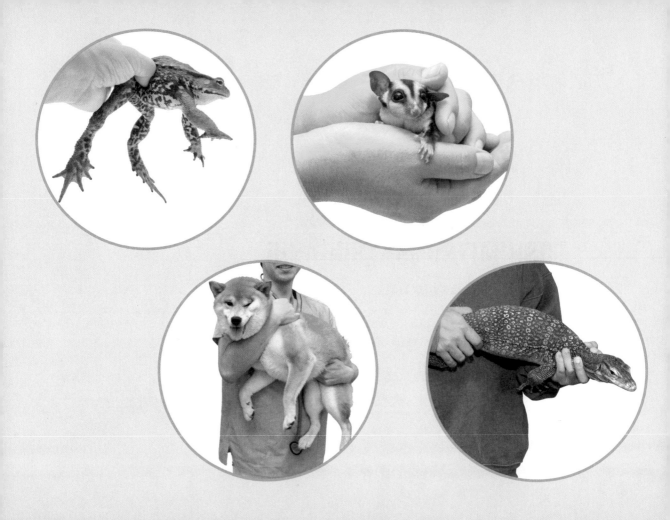

HOW TO HOLD ANIMALS

TOSHIMITSU MATSUHASHI

TRANSLATED BY ANGUS TURVILL

SCRIBNER

NEW YORK   LONDON   TORONTO   SYDNEY   NEW DELHI

Scribner
An Imprint of Simon & Schuster, Inc.
1230 Avenue of the Americas
New York, NY 10020

This Scribner hardcover edition November 2020

SCRIBNER and design are registered trademarks of The Gale Group, Inc., used under license by Simon & Schuster, Inc., the publisher of this work.

For information about special discounts for bulk purchases, please contact Simon & Schuster Special Sales at 1-866-506-1949 or business@simonandschuster.com.

The Simon & Schuster Speakers Bureau can bring authors to your live event. For more information or to book an event, contact the Simon & Schuster Speakers Bureau at 1-866-248-3049 or visit our website at www.simonspeakers.com.

Manufactured in the United States of America

10 9 8 7 6 5 4 3 2 1

Library of Congress Cataloging-in-Publication Data has been applied for.

ISBN 978-1-9821-5591-9
ISBN 978-1-9821-5593-3 (ebook)

CONTENTS

INTRODUCTION

Sometimes a beloved dog that you've taken care of for years nips at you when it's not feeling well. A lizard that usually tolerates being held is suddenly aggressive or a snake that the encyclopedia describes as harmless bites you. Or, on the other hand, a spider known to be poisonous crawls right by you.

Every animal has its own particular characteristics—it's not always simply a question of what species it is. However experienced you may be, however brave, however kind, however knowledgeable, when you hold an animal, you are holding an individual creature.

It's important to hold animals in ways that not only keep us safe but also don't harm the animals. Since we coexist with animals, and more often than not, it's we who hold the animals, not the animals who hold us, we are responsible for the manner in which we come into direct contact with them.

HOW TO USE THIS BOOK

This book shows you how specialists in four different fields pick up and hold animals. Their methods are based on their professional experience and careful consideration of the safety of animals and humans.

1. If you are a beginner.

First read this book from start to finish, marking pages that deal with animals you have come across before. When you're done, go back and read those pages again carefully so that you can commit the holding techniques to memory. When you see a familiar animal out in the world, you'll be able to try picking it up with confidence. To help you handle other animals if and when you encounter them for the first time, we recommend you carry this book around with you.

2. If you're experienced.

For the more experienced, we also recommend that you read this book from cover to cover. When you have familiarized yourself with all the ways of holding the animals described here by the experts, think about how they differ from your own methods.

For animals you have held before, decide which approach suits you best. Is it your old one or the one in the book? Which is safer for you and the animal? Try both methods out and compare. For animals in the book you have never before picked up, try out the expert's technique when the opportunity arises.

3. If you can't stand the idea of holding an animal.

Even you should read this book from beginning to end and keep it with you. If ever you're walking along and meet other people having trouble holding an animal, you can flip to the right page and show them how it's done!

4. And whoever you are.

You should always think carefully about picking up any wild animal and supervise children around animals. Be prepared for things to sometimes go wrong. Use common sense and always follow laws and regulations protecting the animals you come across.

Animal Photographer Toshimitsu Matsuhashi Holds Them Like This!

Children seldom try to pick up animals these days. This is not surprising. Their parents belong to a generation that doesn't feel close to nature. They tell their children that wild animals are dangerous. Sad, isn't it?

I don't necessarily mean to suggest that you should try to pick up every animal shown on these pages. A lot of them should be left to professionals. But why not try picking up creatures around you, the ones that are most familiar?

Let's begin there.

PROFILE

Toshimitsu Matsuhashi

After working for many years at an aquarium, Toshimitsu decided to become an animal photographer. He produces children's books using his photos of wildlife.

CREATURES AROUND YOU

GRASSHOPPERS AND CRICKETS

The prothorax is where it's at.

The hardest part of a grasshopper's body is around the prothorax, where the wings start. Pick it up there with your forefinger, or index finger, and thumb. Don't squeeze too tight. Try to apply just the right amount of pressure. This method works for large grasshoppers, such as the oriental long-headed locust.

Grasshoppers and crickets live in grassy areas, riverbeds, gardens, and parks. You keep trying to catch them, but . . . they're awkward to hold. If you grasp the wrong part, you may get bitten, snap off one of its back legs, or hurt it on its spines.

If you're using a net, try to coax the insect into the corner and look its body over carefully to figure out how to pick it up.

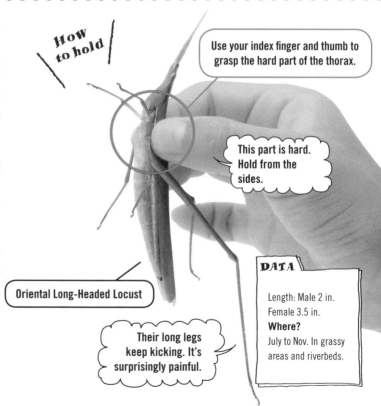

How to hold

Use your index finger and thumb to grasp the hard part of the thorax.

This part is hard. Hold from the sides.

Oriental Long-Headed Locust

Their long legs keep kicking. It's surprisingly painful.

DATA

Length: Male 2 in.
Female 3.5 in.
Where?
July to Nov. In grassy areas and riverbeds.

Holding them by the legs is not advised, but . . .

In general, you shouldn't hold an insect's legs, because there's a risk they'll break. But if you can't judge where to pick up a cricket, then one option is to gently take hold of both back legs together. It's a useful method for crickets that bite, and you can use the same method with any grasshopper-type insect.

This part's hard, but the neck moves, so it's not a good place for holding.

You can hold the legs at the joints.

They're carnivorous, so when they bite, it hurts!

Eastern Bush Cricket

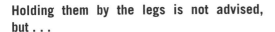

{ How to hold }

DATA

Length: About 1.4 in.
Where?
July to Nov. They sit and "sing" on thick blades of grass in grassy areas and riverbeds.

3

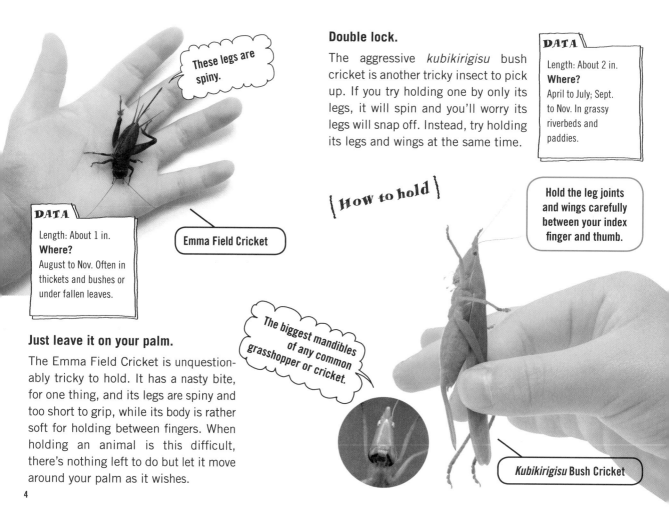

These legs are spiny.

Emma Field Cricket

DATA

Length: About 1 in.
Where?
August to Nov. Often in thickets and bushes or under fallen leaves.

Just leave it on your palm.

The Emma Field Cricket is unquestionably tricky to hold. It has a nasty bite, for one thing, and its legs are spiny and too short to grip, while its body is rather soft for holding between fingers. When holding an animal is this difficult, there's nothing left to do but let it move around your palm as it wishes.

Double lock.

The aggressive *kubikirigisu* bush cricket is another tricky insect to pick up. If you try holding one by only its legs, it will spin and you'll worry its legs will snap off. Instead, try holding its legs and wings at the same time.

DATA

Length: About 2 in.
Where?
April to July; Sept. to Nov. In grassy riverbeds and paddies.

{ How to hold }

Hold the leg joints and wings carefully between your index finger and thumb.

The biggest mandibles of any common grasshopper or cricket.

Kubikirigisu **Bush Cricket**

4

PRAYING MANTISES

Hoodlums of the grass.

A tough, uncompromising character lurking in the undergrowth, the praying mantis looks cool, with an elegant shape and a faintly distracted expression when on the attack. If it were the size of a cat, you wouldn't stand a chance. If it were the size of a human, it would rule the world.

If provoked, a praying mantis will try to attack you with its scythe-like front legs. So your fingers have to duck, sway, and weave like a boxer as they approach. Come at it from behind and aim to get the thorax (the thin part) between your forefinger and thumb. But be careful! The joints of the front legs (the scythes) are flexible, and if your fingers land on the wrong spot, the scythes will hit their mark. Make sure your index finger and thumb are close to the joints. That way, the scythes shouldn't reach you, and you won't be bitten either.

How to hold

Narrow-Winged Mantis

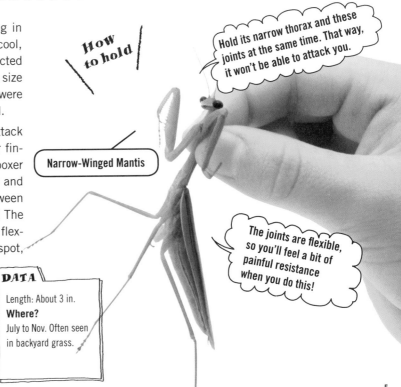

Hold its narrow thorax and these joints at the same time. That way, it won't be able to attack you.

The joints are flexible, so you'll feel a bit of painful resistance when you do this!

DATA

Length: About 3 in.
Where?
July to Nov. Often seen in backyard grass.

DRAGONFLIES

Wings together!

From time immemorial, people have been trying to get dragonflies to land on their index fingers. They gyrate their finger in front of a dragonfly's eyes, as if this will lure the dragonfly onto it. For just as long, dragonflies have been completely ignoring them.

If you are that close to one, there's a better technique. Slowly stretch one hand out underneath the dragonfly. Then, keeping your eyes fixed on its eyes, quickly bring your hands diagonally together from front and back, catching the dragonfly between your palms. Once you've caught it, switch quickly to the standard holding method (described on the next page)—otherwise you'll be bitten.

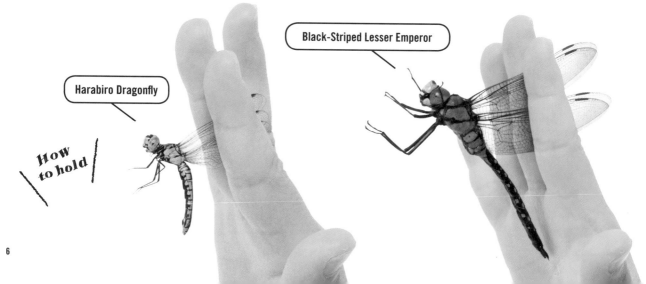

Harabiro Dragonfly

Black-Striped Lesser Emperor

How to hold

The Standard Holding Method for Dragonflies

Dragonflies look cute, so it can come as a surprise to learn that they are committed carnivores! Their bite can be quite painful, so it's best to hold them by their wings. Once you've caught one in a net or your hand, stand their wings up vertically and clasp them between your index and middle fingers. This way you won't get bitten, and the dragonfly's wings won't be damaged.

Globe Skimmer

Konoshime Dragonfly

Golden-Ringed Dragonfly

Mortonagrion Damselfly

BUTTERFLIES

Precious, precious powder.

With their bright colors and slow, floaty movement, you'd think catching butterflies would be a breeze. But they're very good at giving you the slip, and it takes a lot of practice to catch one in a net. Your best-aimed swoosh will often leave them drifting happily away.

Anyone who has held a butterfly before has noticed the powdery residue left on their fingers. This powder (scales, in fact) is vital to butterflies. It not only forms the pattern on their wings but it also helps them to fly in wet weather conditions and slip out of spiders' webs.

When you catch a butterfly, you should always take good care not to damage the scales, whether you're going to keep it as a specimen or let it go.

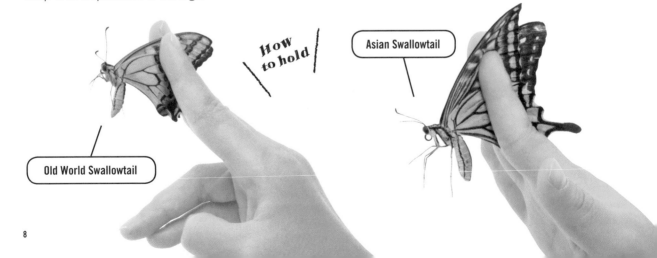

How to hold

Asian Swallowtail

Old World Swallowtail

No fingertips.

If you hold the wings with your finger pads, you're likely to get some sweat or grease on them, which may stick to and dislodge some of the scales. You may also unintentionally rub your fingertips together. So it's best to hold the wings between your index and middle fingers.

Small Copper

Cabbage Butterfly

Chinese Peacock

Common Bluebottle

CRAYFISH

Don't take your eyes off their pincers.

Crayfish sometimes get bad press, but they're a great choice for helping children learn about taking care of animals. They're hardy, interesting specimens to observe, and easy to keep. If all goes well, the female will lay eggs and molt. But they've got sharp pincers, so you'll get hurt if you don't know how to hold them!

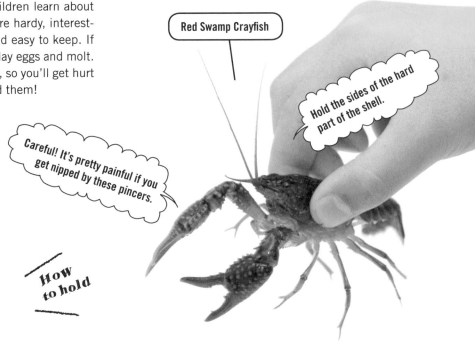

Red Swamp Crayfish

Hold the sides of the hard part of the shell.

Careful! It's pretty painful if you get nipped by these pincers.

How to hold

DATA

Length: About 4.7 in.
Where?
Still parts of rivers and other waterways, as well as wetlands such as paddies, ponds, and bogs.

Perilous pinches.

As long as you keep your eye on the crayfish's pincers, you shouldn't have any problems. Pick the crayfish up from behind by the hard part of its shell. The pincers can't reach you there, but be careful nevertheless. A magnificent pair of large pincers won't be a threat, but if the pincers are small, your fingers may be in range.

CRABS

DANGER: Beware of the coconut crab.

Have you ever felt the irresistible urge to chase after a scurrying crab? It's as though their nimble scamper makes you forget all of your other responsibilities and abandon whatever you're doing. But you must be careful. A spur-of-the-moment decision to follow a crab on the move should be followed by speedy and precise action. Hesitate and the crab may get away, or its pincers may inflict pain like you've never experienced before.

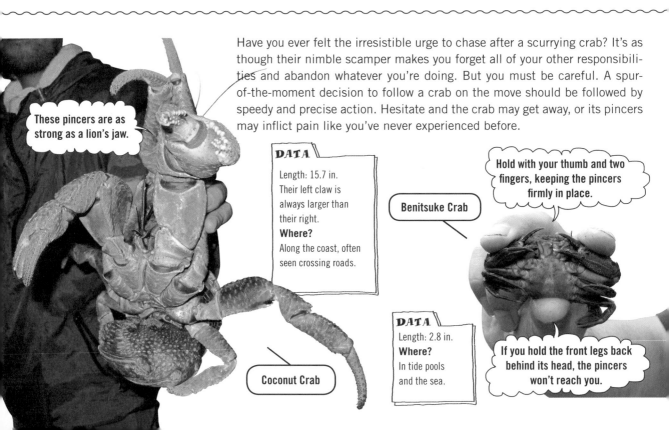

These pincers are as strong as a lion's jaw.

DATA

Length: 15.7 in.
Their left claw is always larger than their right.
Where?
Along the coast, often seen crossing roads.

Coconut Crab

Benitsuke Crab

Hold with your thumb and two fingers, keeping the pincers firmly in place.

DATA

Length: 2.8 in.
Where?
In tide pools and the sea.

If you hold the front legs back behind its head, the pincers won't reach you.

Watch out for the powerful pincers!

The standard way to hold a crab is to use your index finger and thumb to grip the left and right edges of the shell. That's all there is to it. Most crabs, whatever their size, can be held this way. But it won't suit the more aggressive species, like the Benitsuke crab. They'll struggle like mad to get out of your grip, and if you don't let go, they'll catch your cowering fingers between their shell and legs and snap at you with their pincers. To avoid this risk, use a three-point grip, with your thumb at the rear of the shell and your index and middle fingers at the front, keeping the pincers firmly in place.

The most dangerous crab is the coconut crab . . . If you're bitten by one, you can be sure you'll lose more than just a few drops of blood. The coconut crab is a type of hermit crab with a tough exoskeleton rather than a shell, so it's not obvious where to hold it. If you take the front legs (those next to the pincers) and hold them firmly above and behind the pincers, its claws won't be able to move much, allowing you to hold the crab safely.

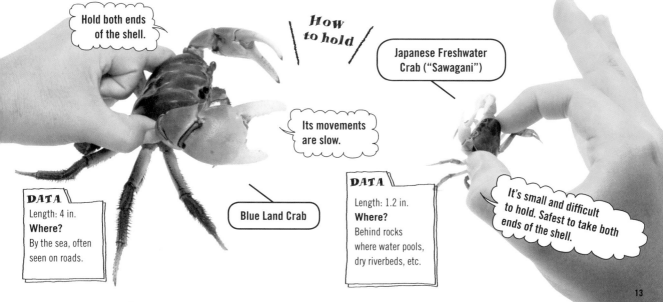

Hold both ends of the shell.

How to hold

Japanese Freshwater Crab ("Sawagani")

Its movements are slow.

DATA
Length: 4 in.
Where?
By the sea, often seen on roads.

Blue Land Crab

DATA
Length: 1.2 in.
Where?
Behind rocks where water pools, dry riverbeds, etc.

It's small and difficult to hold. Safest to take both ends of the shell.

SNAILS AND SLUGS

Their tentacles have eyes!

These slimy characters are among the most frequently encountered of our fellow creatures. You may be worried about slugs as pests in the garden or perhaps the children want to keep a snail as a pet. Even if you don't find the idea of picking them up enticing, it's probably best to know how to.

How to hold

There are eyes at the ends of the two large tentacles, but they don't see very well.

Small tentacle

Misuji Maimai Snail
(Japanese garden snail)

It breathes through this hole.

The shell is surprisingly soft.

DATA

Length: About 1.7 in.
Where?
April to Nov. On leaves
when it's rainy, or
on concrete walls.
Endemic to Japan.

Slime avoidance.

Picking up a snail is easy. Just grasp the shell between your thumb and forefinger. The shell is fragile, so be careful not to squeeze it. The slime (mucus) that snails secrete when moving can be slippery, so don't get any on your fingers. If you give the shell a little shake, the snail will retreat inside. However, it's hard to avoid slime with slugs, so try picking them up with wooden chopsticks.

Use chopsticks . . . but don't eat it!

How to hold

Three-Band Garden Slug

If it gets super slimy, it'll be difficult to pick up even with chopsticks.

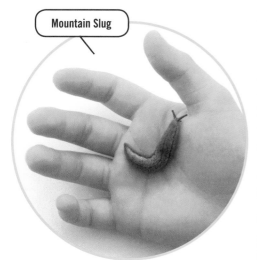

Mountain Slug

The mountain slug, found, where else?, in the mountains, is about four inches long and difficult to pick up with chopsticks. So there's nothing to do but take a deep breath and put it in the palm of your hand . . . or, I suppose, you could always just leave it where it is.

DATA

Length: Around 2 in.
Where?
Year-round, under planters and in gardens.

15

FROGS AND TOADS

Some are poisonous. All are handsome.

Japanese Toad

Glands here secrete poison. Don't touch them!

It's not a good jumper, but it moves quickly and has a powerful kick.

DATA

Length: About 6 in.
Where?
April to Nov. Pops up in woods and gardens.

People feel nervous about picking up frogs. They assume frogs will be too quick to catch, for one thing. And they worry that frog skin is delicate, or that frogs are so small they'll get squashed in the process of catching them. Some folks believe the heat of human flesh can burn frogs. But actually, these amphibians are tough. They sit happily in the scalding sun, and tadpoles can live in water that feels hot to the touch. Of course, you shouldn't squash them or pull on their legs, or walk around for too long with one in your hands. And for your safety, remember to wash your hands thoroughly afterwards.

Toxic toads.

Toads secrete a white sticky poisonous fluid from the parotid glands behind their eyes when they sense danger. It can appear on their backs too. When holding a toad, it's best to avoid these parts and grip its belly instead. If it looks like it's going to start squirming, wrap one hand around its back legs.

Japanese Wrinkled Frog

Tokyo Daruma Pond Frog

Japanese Tree Frog

Mind the wrinkles.

Unlike other frogs, which are more slippery, you can pick up wrinkled frogs with a finger and thumb on each flank thanks to their skin's rough texture. Once you're holding them, they often stop moving. You can try this method with other frog species, but there's a greater risk of dropping them.

DATA

Length: 1.5 in.
Where?
April to Oct. They like flowing water—anything from an irrigation channel to a mountain stream.

No jumping!

Tokyo Daruma pond frogs, black-spotted frogs, and Japanese brown frogs are all great jumpers and can be hard to handle if you don't hold them properly. If one starts kicking, you might drop it or accidentally hurt its legs. You should hold it firmly with your hand wrapped around its belly and back legs.

DATA

Length: 2.3 in.
Where?
May to Sept. Around marshlands and paddies.

Between the palms.

Tree frogs often sit on leaves. Approach quietly, and with both hands pick one up with the leaf it's sitting on, and hold it between your palms. When you feel the frog moving onto your hand, you can gently remove the leaf. Hold your hands so that there is as much space between your palms as possible. This method is good for various other small frogs too, including the Japanese gliding frog.

DATA

Length: 1.6 in.
Where?
April to Nov. In the grass, near paddies, etc.

17

LIZARDS

They are not morning people!

You see lizards near the house and in the garden, and you want to catch them . . . but they're so quick! The key is in the timing—time of day, that is. Lizards move fast once their bodies have been warmed by the sun, so get to them before they've had a chance to sunbathe. In spring and autumn, this means before 9:00 a.m. In summer, try before 7:00 a.m. When picking them up, it's important not to touch their tails. Lizards and geckos all flick their tails when they sense danger, and then run off.

Catch geckos at night.

Geckos live in cracks in walls and in shutter casings. At night they come out to eat insects that gather around the lights at your front door and windows. When you see one, approach it slowly and then snap it up in the same way described for lizards. Geckos are flat, so don't hold their sides. Instead, hold from the top and bottom, near their head. Make sure you don't squeeze their throats.

Schlegel's Japanese Gecko

DATA

Length: About 7.8 in.
Where?
April to Nov. In gardens and outside houses. On concrete in the morning sun.

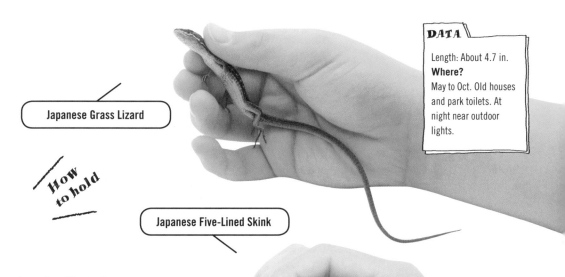

Japanese Grass Lizard

DATA

Length: About 4.7 in.
Where?
May to Oct. Old houses
and park toilets. At
night near outdoor
lights.

How to hold

Japanese Five-Lined Skink

DATA

Length: About 7.8 in.
Where?
April to Nov. In the
sun on concrete or
rocks near houses or
paddies.

Remain calm, cool, and collected.

A lizard that has just come out to lie in the sun has one priority—to warm up. It won't run off until the last moment. Approach it with a nonchalant air, as if you had not the slightest interest in catching it. Even if it runs off once, it will soon come back. Just keep still and wait. When it comes out, bring your hand down quickly over its whole body so that its head is between your thumb and forefinger. If all goes well, you can pick it up by bringing your finger and thumb together around the top of its neck.

SNAKES

Not for the faint of heart.

When you come across a snake, be extremely careful. If you don't know what type of snake it is, it's best to keep your distance. But if you definitely know what type it is, it's only natural to want to have a go at picking it up to appreciate it more closely.

Not all rat snakes are harmless.

Though rat snakes can grow to over six and a half feet long, they have a reputation for docility. However, I myself have been bitten by rat snakes many times. Snakebites lead to their own set of complications and hazards, so always approach these snakes with the expectation that you may be bitten. Bring your hand down in one movement over its head and grab its neck. Then wrap its tail over your arm.

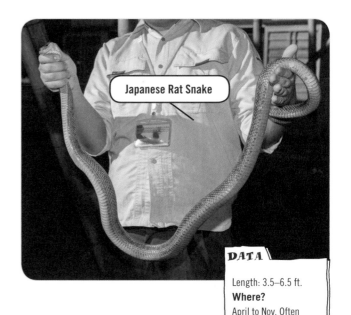

Japanese Rat Snake

DATA

Length: 3.5–6.5 ft.
Where?
April to Nov. Often seen near houses, basking in the morning sunshine.

How about a poisonous one?

The tiger keelback is quite docile, and I've never been bitten by one. But its poison is powerful, so this snake should never be picked up. Well, I say that, but I have actually picked one up myself. When I was holding it, I made sure I had control of its head.

Tiger Keelback

Approach Procedure: Young Snakes

When it's in a position that makes it easy to pick up . . . **1**

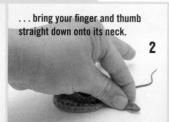

. . . bring your finger and thumb straight down onto its neck. **2**

Hold the sides of its jaws between your finger and thumb and lift. **3**

Take the rest of the snake into your hand. **4**

A WORD FROM THE EXPERT

Before you pick up any creature you come across in the great outdoors . . .

You have to make a judgment about whether it's really okay to do so. Unless you are an expert or work with animals, it's difficult to remember information about lots of different creatures. Even mushroom experts sometimes eat poisonous mushrooms. You think you know, but you may make a mistake. If you don't really know, or if you feel uncertain, don't pick the animal up. Admitting you're not sure is sometimes the brave thing to do.

As a photographer, I come across a lot of animals, but unless it's really necessary, in a studio shoot for example, I don't go out of my way to pick them up. And of course I never touch an animal I don't know about. This keeps me safe, and avoids trouble for whoever is with me.

Let's imagine I'm on an island with someone who gets bitten by a poisonous snake.

We've been on the island for a few hours. We've driven along happily photographing snakes as we go. We reach a park. We split up to see what we can find. Before long I hear a voice in the distance calling my name.

I'm concentrating on my photography, so I ignore it.

After a while I go back to the car and find my colleague there. "I found a snake," she says. "I thought you'd want to see it so I picked it up. Then it bit me."

"Oh dear! How nice of you. I'm so sorry . . ." Then I see a large pit viper in her right hand!

"That's a pit viper," I say. "Throw it as far away as you can!" Then I get the poison extractor kit from my camera bag and try sucking the poison from the wound, but it feels dry and I don't think I've got the poison out. That's not surprising. It's already been ten minutes since I heard her calling to me. It's no use. We'll have to find a clinic. According to the map, the nearest is twenty minutes away by car. We drive frantically to the clinic, only to find it's closed down. The next nearest clinic is another thirty minutes away.

My companion's almost in tears. "It's okay," I say. "We'll get there soon!" I drive as fast as I can and get to the hospital in twenty minutes. But by now it's almost an hour since she was bitten. Her arm is swollen right up to the shoulder!

She's taken straight into a treatment room. She comes out after having serum and an intravenous drip, with her swollen arm wrapped thickly with bandages. Of course, the next day's fieldwork and photography sessions are canceled. And she has to visit the hospital for days afterwards. She has a fever the whole time we are on the island. It's a nightmare!

So . . . I'm very safety conscious. Turn the page to see the equipment I always bring with me when I photograph animals.

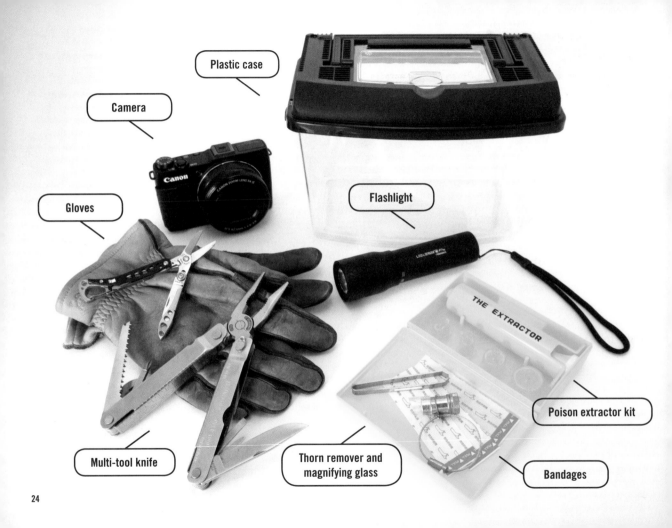

Plastic case

Camera

Gloves

Flashlight

Multi-tool knife

Thorn remover and
magnifying glass

Poison extractor kit

Bandages

THE EXTRACTOR

PEACE OF MIND IN A BAG

Camera

Photographs are useful records. Always carry a high-quality compact digital camera and take photos of the creatures you see. Then, if someone gets bitten, you'll have vital information at hand. You won't have to catch the creature and take it with you to be certain about identification.

Gloves

When handling potentially dangerous snakes or caterpillars, always wear Kevlar or strong leather gloves.

Multi-tool knife

A lot of people carry pocketknives, but in the field the most useful tools tend to be pliers and scissors. So have a strong plier-style knife (*right*) and a scissor-style knife (*left*).

Plastic case

This is for carrying creatures that you've caught and want to take home. If you're bitten by a snake, you can put it in the case and take it with you to the hospital.

Flashlight

Flashlights are not just for camping trips and power outages. They're great for seeing into dark places anywhere, anytime and for examining bites, for example.

Poison extractor kit

This tool extracts poison from a bite. Place over the wound and suck out the poison.

Thorn remover and magnifying glass

Useful for plant thorns, insect stings, etc.

Bandages

Essential for cuts and bites.

Pet Shop Owner Takahiro Goto Holds Them Like This!

Shops like mine stock all sorts of animals. Everything must be kept clean, and that includes the animal boxes and showcases. When we're cleaning those out, it's important to properly and quickly pick up the animals that inhabit them. We also have to hold the animals when we show them to customers. And then we have to advise customers on how to look after them, including how to pick them up and hold them.

So our dual priorities are safety, for both handler and animal, and operational efficiency. Together these underlie what we call our "rational" approach to holding animals.

PROFILE

Takahiro Goto

From Hanamaki, Iwate Prefecture,
northern Japan
Takahiro runs a pet shop. He also pays
regular visits to the local paddies to check
all is well. He is an expert in both pets and
the natural word.

INSECTS, ARACHNIDS, AND UNUSUAL PETS

SCORPIONS

Watch out for the danger triangle!

Madras Forest Scorpion

Many scorpion species found in the wild are normally not poisonous enough to pose a threat to human life. Nor are the types that are commonly kept as pets. But some scorpions are extremely poisonous. What if you happen to see a scorpion crawling into a friend's bed? What would you do?

DATA

Where?
Forests of South Asia, India.
Yellow-legged are said to be the largest type of scorpion.

This is the poisonous stinger.

The stinger is curved like a fishhook, designed to catch anything in front of it. So it is best to approach from behind.

The most dangerous zone is the triangle between the claws and the stinger.

Triangular danger zone

The claws look dangerous, but actually they're not capable of inflicting much pain.

Approach Procedure: Scorpions

1 Approach softly from behind.

2 Take the stinger quickly between thumb and finger.

3 Lift.

Control the stinger.

When picking up a scorpion be wary of the poisonous stinger. As long as you are in control of the stinger, there's no danger. Don't fret if the scorpion is waving its claws about. Just keep hold of the stinger. If the scorpion won't stop moving, you can try to calm it down by holding out your free hand in front of it to attract its attention.

Emperor Scorpion

How to hold

DATA

Where?
Central Africa.
The most common pet scorpion. Strong, with large claws, the venom of adults is not lethal to humans.

Swing.

If it bends its body upwards, swing it gently back and forth.

29

TARANTULAS

Moving and grooving.

Chilean Rose Tarantula

Let a tarantula walk freely on your palm. If it looks like it's going to climb up your arm, hold out your other hand so that it walks there instead.

{ How to hold }

Keep still and let it forget all about you.

Angry!

Angry!

Angry!

It's best not to be too pushy when dealing with a tarantula. Just put out your hand and let it climb on of its own accord. If it gets angry, it will be impossible to deal with, and some types are very short-tempered. If you feel it's getting difficult to handle, guide it towards its plastic case. If it's angry, contain it with the top and wait until it calms down.

A lost cause. If it looks like this, give up!

Like scorpions, tarantulas have a reputation for being dangerous, but only some species are poisonous enough to pose a direct threat to human lives. Unlike scorpions, tarantulas have the disagreeable habit of lurking up in trees and other high places. They also have rather unpredictable patterns of movement. Some shoot out poisonous bristles that can cause an allergic reaction if you touch them. Conventional wisdom says to leave a tarantula be: "Just because you see one, that doesn't mean it's going to attack." But hold on! What if you see a tarantula climbing up a loved one's back? Better learn how to handle them just in case!

DATA

Where?
Deserts in Bolivia and Chile.
A well-behaved tarantula normally moves slowly but is quick when hunting.

Some types shoot out bristles from here.

Be careful of its mandibles!

Approach Procedure: Tarantulas

1 Guide it towards your hand.

2 Get it onto your hand.

3 Keep your hand still as it climbs on.

4 Once it's on, you can move.

LARGE STAG BEETLES

Check out those mandibles.

Stag beetles' "antlers" are mandibles that move, and getting your finger stuck between them can be pretty painful. Figuring out where to hold a stag beetle presents some difficulty because there are hundreds of varieties with mandibles of different sizes and shapes.

What if you're on a family vacation and you find a stag beetle lying in wait by the window of the hotel? "Catch it!" your son says. Do you want to be someone who replies, "Uh, well, I'm not really much good at that sort of thing"? Probably not. Better to be prepared by learning a tried-and-true method.

DATA

Length: 2–4 in.
Where?
Southeast Asia.
Mandibles come in a variety of shapes, and you can easily confuse one species for another.

DATA

Length: 2–4 in.
Where?
Southeast Asia.
They're not that strong, but if they get your finger, it really hurts!

Stag beetles have mandibles that vary in size and shape.

Hold in one of these two places.

Alces Stag Beetle

Didieri Stag Beetle

If it looks like this, call it a day!

Quick thinking and intuition.

Stag beetles should normally be held between your thumb and forefinger on the prothorax or metathorax. If you're trying to clean the beetle's box and it rears up aggressively, you may not have enough space to get at the prothorax from behind. Instead, try to get control of the beetle's most powerful weapons—its mandibles. The best approach will vary according to the shape and the stance of the beetle. You will need to rely on your beetle intuition.

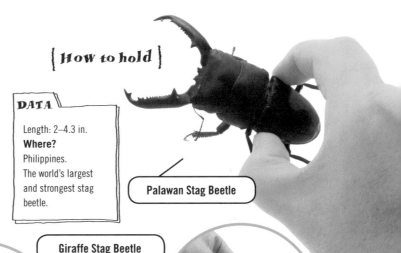

{ How to hold }

DATA

Length: 2–4.3 in.
Where?
Philippines.
The world's largest and strongest stag beetle.

Palawan Stag Beetle

Variations in holding methods

Giraffe Stag Beetle

DATA

Length: 2–4.7 in.
Where?
Southeast Asia and India.
A flat beetle with mandibles that are very long for its body.

Suitable for types with long mandibles.

If it assumes an aggressive stance, pick it up from the front, holding both sides near the mandibles.

If it's very angry and you can't do anything else, you can try holding it like this.

33

COCKROACHES AND MILLIPEDES

Are you up for the challenge?

Keep still.

Round-Backed Millipede

Two of the world's most notorious creepy-crawlies—the cockroach and the millipede! "No way am I picking up one of those" you may say, but then how are you going to protect your home from these noxious pests? Squash millipedes with tissues? Bash cockroaches with a rolled-up newspaper? Spray the place with insecticide? If you squash millipedes, there's a nasty smell. What will you do with a flattened cockroach? And you certainly don't want insecticide all over the upholstery, do you? Well then, here's a different method to try.

Prevent the stench.

Millipedes don't bite and they're not quick, but they do emit a foul-smelling fluid to repel enemies. If you gently encourage the millipede to climb onto your hand and then shake it a little, it will roll up into a protective coil and won't produce a smell.

Madagascar Hissing Cockroach

How to hold

If it's a fast cockroach, use a three-point hold, with a thumb and two fingers.

Yaeyama-madara Cockroach

Don't think of it as a cockroach.

Cockroaches are quick to scurry away and hide, so they are often elusive. When one is spotted, your family won't leave you alone until you find it again and you yourself won't be able to relax either. To avoid such an ordeal, catch the cockroach in your hand from the get-go.

Their bodies and wings are soft, so don't hold cockroaches by their sides. Hold them gently with your thumb on top and fingers underneath. The trick is to imagine what you're holding is not a cockroach at all but something more palatable, like a cricket.

LONG-TAILED CHINCHILLAS

The world's most adorable rodents.

Chinchillas are rodents from the Andes whose cute appearance has made them popular as pets. They have the densest fur of any land mammal. Imagine you're in love with someone who works in a pet shop. You're in there one day pretending to browse, when a chinchilla escapes. Your crush asks you to catch it . . . Obviously you want to look cool and competent. So be prepared. Now's your chance to learn how to handle a chinchilla.

Chinchillas are gentle creatures, but if they're not used to humans, they will become agitated. Hold them firmly at the back of the neck so that they realize that acting up will get them nowhere. With your other hand hold their rear legs. Adjust the strength of your grip accordingly. If you hold chinchillas too loosely, they may squirm and fall. If your grip is too strong, it will cause them undue stress.

DATA

Length: 11.8 in.
Where:
Chile.
Known as a lab test animal and for its high-quality, thick fur.

Its big ears look worthy of a cartoon character.

They're good at standing up on their hind legs.

How to hold

CHIPMUNKS

Chubby-cheeked tricksters.

Some time ago chipmunks were well established as pets, but for various reasons the numbers imported to Japan have fallen sharply in recent years. They are usually friendly and can be trained to stay in your hand. However, they belong to the same family as squirrels, and squirrels are generally tricky to deal with. Chipmunks have sharp and powerful teeth that can gnaw through wood, so if you get bitten, there will be blood and the wound may be deep. The key is to master how to hold them and then gradually build a relationship of trust.

Pick a chipmunk up by the loose fur at the back of its neck.

DATA

Length: 7–7.8 in.
Where?
Asia.
Import restrictions mean it's not as common a pet as it used to be.
They can be very unruly.

A chipmunk may have a cute face, but if it isn't used to humans and you suddenly put your hand out to pick it up, you'll get bitten. To start off on a better note, pick it up between your thumb and forefinger, pinching the loose skin at the back of its neck and letting the chipmunk hang down. Some people think this is cruel, but the skin at the back of their necks is like the skin on human elbows. You can stretch it a bit without it hurting.

SUGAR GLIDERS

The sweetest faces. Until you hear their cry.

Sugar gliders are becoming popular pets. With their big ears and round eyes, they can easily capture a child's heart. But getting them to behave as you want them to behave is no simple matter. They are supple, active, and agile critters. And they bite. They refuse to stay still in your hand, and whenever you try restraining them, they'll let out an unearthly cry you'd hardly think possible given their size. Nevertheless, as some parents know, when a child wants something, he or she must have it. So learn how to hold these small gliding marsupials for when it comes time to welcome one to your home as a pet.

{ How to hold }

DATA

Length: 6–7.8 in.
Where?
Indonesia and Australia. Young stay in the mother's pouch for about seventy days after birth. Sugar gliders have gliding membranes that allow them to glide up to 164 feet.

Even pet shop owners want them to keep still!

When a suger glider is not used to humans, it's best to hold it firmly around the body and neck. But beware, if you restrain it too much it will let out a terrible scream. We pet shop owners prefer customers not to witness such resistance from creatures they are considering taking home with them. We try to overcome our fear of being bitten and, repressing our desire to pin the creature down, we cup it between our palms. The sugar glider seems to feel secure there and usually settles down. If you are responsive and don't exert too much pressure, you'll probably be able to hold your sugar glider like this without problems.

The vet wraps it in a towel.

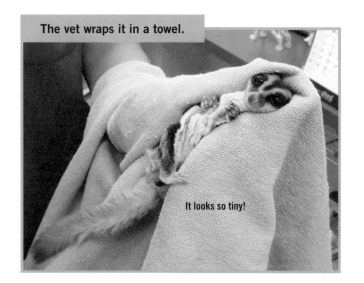

It looks so tiny!

This is how a vet holds one!

HAMSTERS

Some bite—some don't . . .

Hamsters have become desirable pets in Japan ever since they were featured in a popular TV animation series called *Hamtaro*. In the past people saw them as an unusual pet to have, but now they are quite common. Many zoos have areas where children can have direct contact with animals, and hamsters are often included in these miniature menageries.

If your son or daughter says, "Daddy! I want to pet the hamster!" the correct response isn't "Well, I'm not going to touch it!" The correct response is "Sure, look, kiddo, this is how to hold it!"

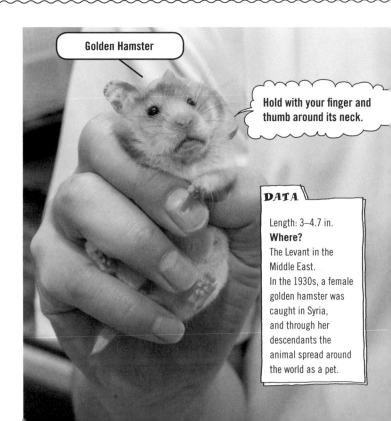

Golden Hamster

Hold with your finger and thumb around its neck.

DATA

Length: 3–4.7 in.
Where?
The Levant in the Middle East.
In the 1930s, a female golden hamster was caught in Syria, and through her descendants the animal spread around the world as a pet.

So small!

Hamsters are small and often sweet-tempered. Many will sit happily in your palm. For safety, it's probably best to hold them between cupped palms.

DATA

Length: 2.3–3 in.
Where?
Siberia, northern China.
It's called "dwarf" because it's smaller than the golden hamster and "winter white" because its fur turns white in winter.

Winter White Dwarf Hamster

{ How to hold }

The bite test.

Golden hamsters like people, but some are more inclined to bite than others, particularly when woken from a nap. When you first pick one up, hold it from both sides at the back of its neck. Once you've held it a few times, you will know whether it bites or not. If it's a biter, continue to hold it this way. If it's not, cup it in your hands.

FANCY MICE

Just like a cartoon!

The tail is strong and can easily support the weight of the body.

How to hold

Unless you give a mouse a nasty surprise, it won't bite you. They like humans and they're clever. You can carry them in both hands, or in just one.

Tall tails.

When cleaning their boxes, it's most efficient to pick them up by their tails. Some people think this is cruel, but as long as you don't hold them like that for a long time, it doesn't hurt them. Holding them by the tail means there's no chance of their running away. If you don't like doing this, you can hold the mouse in your palm instead and keep a grip on its tail at the same time.

DATA

Length: 2.3–2.7 in.
Where?
Mice are found all over the world.
Fancy mice are various breeds of house mice.

What we call a panda mouse in Japan—because of its panda-like markings—is said to have been bred in the Edo period (1603–1868).

They breed easily and their numbers soon grow. It is said that if one person has a panda mouse, it won't be long before all their friends and neighbors have one too.

If you keep hold of its tail, it won't move much.

This is the mouse secret.

CHICKENS

Fierce poultry.

If you've ever fought with a chicken, you'll know how fierce they are. They attack with their feet and rip your trousers with their spurs. They dodge your counterattack and then, with their formidable beaks, lay straight into any weak spot. If you want to be able to pick up a truly savage chicken, develop your strategies by practicing on the more docile varieties found in pet shops.

One movement.

When it comes to holding chickens, you must first hide your intent. Approach the rooster or hen nonchalantly. As you get closer, it will turn to walk away. Now's your chance—pick it up from behind, placing your hands quickly and firmly over its wings. The secret is to get it done in one fell swoop.

DATA

Length: 15.7–19.7 in.
Where?
All over the world. Domesticated in Southeast Asia and China and then spread to Europe. Guinness World Records lists a variety of hen that produces more than three hundred eggs a year.

Chick = baseball?

Hold a chick as you would a baseball. Grasp the whole chick, with your hand gently wrapped around both sides from the neck downwards. When held this way, the chick will be calm, with a slightly dazed expression.

A WORD FROM THE EXPERT

How to get a rhinoceros beetle off your hand.

Rhinoceros beetles are hugely popular pets in Japan. They're not just found in the woods, but in city-center parks too. A rhinoceros beetle has long claws to keep its large body steady on trees. It's tough to get the beetle to move when its claws are sunken into the skin of your hand. If you try to pull, you'll draw blood. But if you treat it gently and use your mighty human brain, you'll be okay.

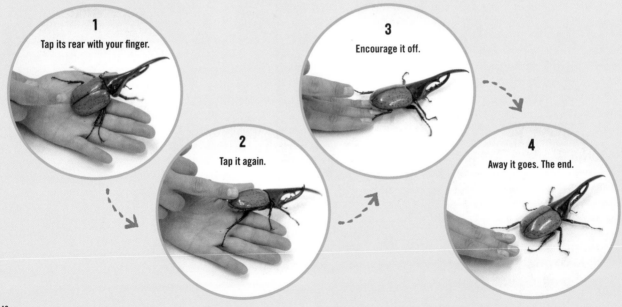

1
Tap its rear with your finger.

2
Tap it again.

3
Encourage it off.

4
Away it goes. The end.

A simple way to get an angry stag beetle out of its plastic box.

When you try to get a stag beetle out to clean its small plastic box, assuming you keep it in one, the beetle often gets cross and starts waving its mandibles about so that you can't slip your hand inside. You begin to despair that you'll never get the box clean.

In that situation, try this:

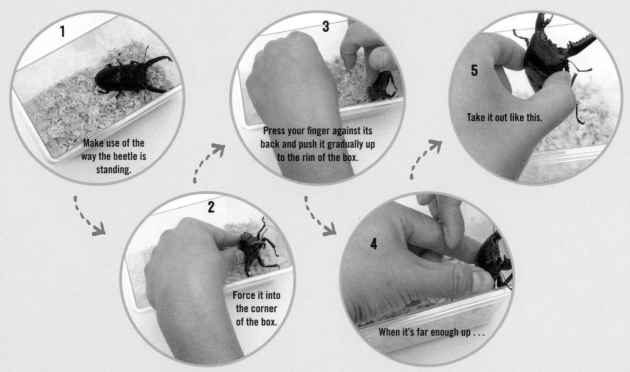

1 Make use of the way the beetle is standing.

2 Force it into the corner of the box.

3 Press your finger against its back and push it gradually up to the rim of the box.

4 When it's far enough up . . .

5 Take it out like this.

49

Veterinarian Kenichi Tamukai Holds Them Like This!

As a veterinarian, my policy is to treat whatever animal is in need.

If I were to tell desperate owners who bring their animals to me, "We can't deal with one of those," or "I don't think I can pick that up," they wouldn't be very happy, would they?

When an animal is in front of me, I try to think of all possibilities and then choose the most suitable method.

I've loved animals since I was small, and of course I feel confident holding all kinds. I'm also a wrestling fan, so I'm familiar with ways of keeping them under control when necessary.

As a vet it's not only a question of holding an animal, I also must keep it still so that I can treat it. This involves having what I call Hold Spirit—a state of mind that helps me keep an animal still in a safe and appropriate way. They say success as a vet is 80 percent a matter of keeping the animals still.

PROFILE

Kenichi Tamukai

Head of the Denen Chofu Veterinary Clinic in southern Tokyo, dealing with dogs and cats, rabbits, reptiles, pigs, sheep, and others. Kenichi has handled two hundred species to date.

PET MAMMALS AND BIRDS

DOGS

Small, medium, and large—there's a right way for each.

Nowadays, pet dog culture sometimes means neatly dressed people venturing out in the morning before the tarmac heats up and strolling gracefully along with their dogs in their arms. A dog is no longer something that must have its everyday walk—it's the owners' valued partner in *their* walk. If it's looking tired or hot, it must be picked up and carried!?

Well, since we can't deny the ever-changing nature of culture, for the good of your back and to avoid risks to the dog, why not learn how the experts do it?

Great Pyrenees

DATA
Length: 16–39 in.
Character:
The king of pets.
Man's best friend.

Large dogs.

Many owners of big dogs hold them by their bottoms with their front legs over one shoulder. But the dog may be difficult to control if it starts wriggling when held like that. If the dog falls, it may hit the ground awkwardly and painfully, and this method can strain both your back and the dog's back. The safest way to carry a big dog is to hold it in both arms as shown in the picture. One arm goes around the top of its front legs, and the other around the top of its back legs. Held in this way, the dog keeps its usual posture, and you can control its whole body. If it starts slipping, you can let it down gently onto the ground into a natural standing position.

Medium-sized dogs.

Hold a medium-sized dog the same way as you hold a large dog. Use a scooping movement to pick it up with one arm around its chest, at the top of its front legs, and one arm around its rear, at the top of its back legs. You may be tempted to carry a medium-sized dog with its front legs over one arm, but if the dog kicks with its front legs, it could fall forwards.

Shiba Inu

When held by its owner, a dog usually makes itself comfortable. With me, they are always held firmly, even if the effort produces an odd expression on my face—or the dog's.

Miniature Dachshund

Small dogs.

For large and medium-sized dogs, it's vital to hold the dogs firmly and securely, but for small dogs, your hold can be gentler—like a cradle. It's important to keep control of the back legs and hold the dog reasonably tightly—this makes it feel secure and calm.

CATS

Some cats are cuddlers. Some are not. All cats do as they please.

Many cats used to live freely, going out when they felt like it and coming back for food whenever they wanted. A cat with a collar and bell belonged to somebody; without a collar and bell, it was assumed to be a street cat. Otherwise there wasn't much difference. But since the 1980s, pet cats' living environments have changed quite a lot.

Nowadays most cats live indoors and their relationship with their owners has become closer. Are you holding yours the right way? Let's check.

How to hold

House Cat

DATA

Length: 11.8–15.7 in.
Character:
Enjoys solitude, but when the mood strikes, likes to be coddled and spoiled.

Cat cradle.

Take the cat in your arms from both sides. Have one hand on the cat's back and the other beneath its bottom, holding its rear legs. The cat will make itself comfortable and be easy to hold. Their living environment may have changed, but cats are still capricious. Some don't like to be cuddled, so don't force them. For situations where you really have to keep them under firm control, see A Word from the Expert on page 73.

How to hold

57

FERRETS

Whole lotta personality.

The ferret's appeal lies in its cute face and mannerisms, as well as its independent, self-reliant spirit. In the past, they weren't popular pets due to their aggressive behavior and strong musky smell. Almost all ferrets for sale these days have had their scent glands removed, and they've been selected for easy temperaments. Even so, if you've encountered their smell, or been bitten by a ferret, you'll no doubt be on your guard. This holding method will come to your aid.

How they're held in pet shops.

When customers are looking at a ferret in a shop, the animal's movements don't have to be controlled too much, so it's often held by its chest with its front legs hanging down, or simply placed on the shop assistant's arm. Held this way, a ferret can be difficult to control if it gets excited. While it sure looks cute when it's acting unruly, if it starts squirming, shift your grip to the back of its neck.

DATA

Length: 11.8–15.7 in.
Character:
Carnivorous, but with a sweet tooth. Cheerful and carefree. Active, but sleeps a lot.

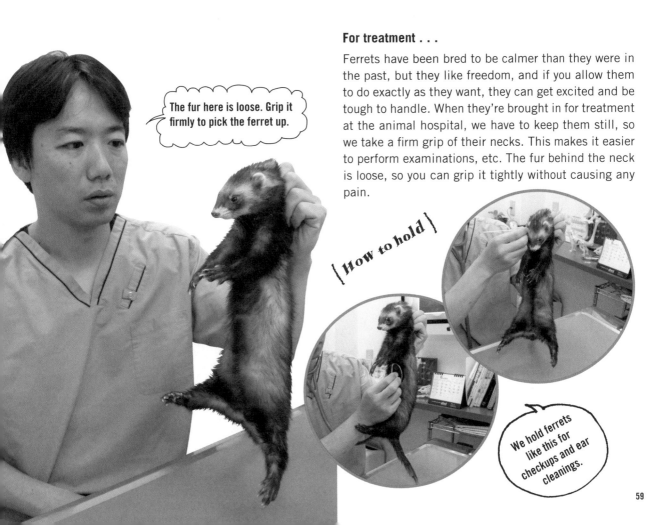

For treatment . . .

Ferrets have been bred to be calmer than they were in the past, but they like freedom, and if you allow them to do exactly as they want, they can get excited and be tough to handle. When they're brought in for treatment at the animal hospital, we have to keep them still, so we take a firm grip of their necks. This makes it easier to perform examinations, etc. The fur behind the neck is loose, so you can grip it tightly without causing any pain.

The fur here is loose. Grip it firmly to pick the ferret up.

{ How to hold }

We hold ferrets like this for checkups and ear cleanings.

RABBITS

Hugs from behind.

Are rabbits always sweet and gentle? No. Many hate being touched by humans. If you approach them in a way that startles or intimidates them, they may bite you with their sharp front teeth. And don't underestimate the power of their back-leg kick—they can jump out of your hold only to land on the ground and risk breaking a bone.

Don't force your desire to cuddle onto a rabbit. Pay attention to its reaction.

DATA

Length: 11.8–23.6 in.
Character:
Timid, and when they're in a bad mood, they stamp the ground. Good at getting attention.

The standard way to hold.

Lop-Eared Rabbit

This is how rabbits are held in pet shops and at home. If you hold them tight against your stomach, they will feel secure and probably remain calm.

First take hold of the soft fur behind its ears and pull up.

Put your hand underneath the rabbit and support its back legs near its bottom.

Carry to a safe place.

...

The natural way to hold a rabbit is with one hand under the rabbit's bottom, the other on its back, and its tummy against yours. But if it gets upset, its back legs can give a powerful kick. To be on the safe side at animal hospitals, rabbits are held from behind, with their backs against the holder's front. One hand goes under the front legs, keeping the chest area still, while the other hand supports the animal under its bottom. If the rabbit is facing the front, any kicks will be in the air and won't really interfere with treatment.

Adjust the rabbit's position.

Silver Marten Rabbit

PARAKEETS

Use a baseball grip.

Pitching a fastball?

Small birds like parakeets and Java sparrows are light and have delicate bones, and it's easy to cause injury when holding them. It's important that they get used to perching on your hands from a very young age. But when they fly off around the room and don't come back, or when you want to take them to the vet, you may have to catch them.

DATA

Length: 7–9 in.
Character:
Likes people. Chatty.
Females often
experience egg binding.

Hold the whole body. Have one finger on each side of the neck.

Sometimes a parakeet will act up when you put your hand inside its cage. Don't take your hand out—just wait for an opportunity, holding your hand out as though you were going to pitch a baseball. When the bird's wings are furled, take hold of it gently from behind. Once its neck is between your forefinger and middle finger, it won't resist.

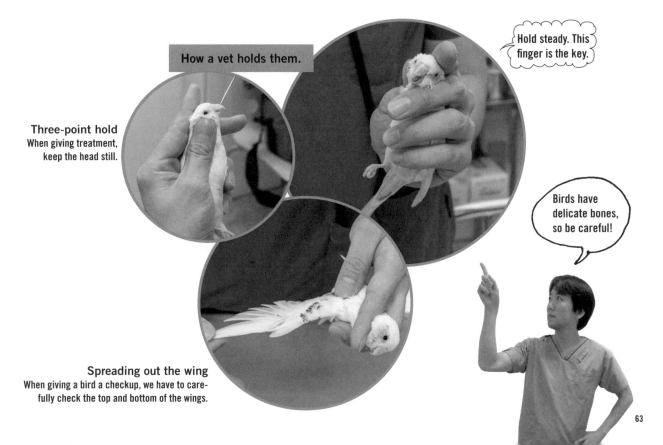

How a vet holds them.

Hold steady. This finger is the key.

Three-point hold
When giving treatment, keep the head still.

Birds have delicate bones, so be careful!

Spreading out the wing
When giving a bird a checkup, we have to carefully check the top and bottom of the wings.

SUNDA SCOPS OWLS

Hold it as gently as a newborn baby.

With woods being destroyed for housing, the number of scops owls is in decline. But some live undeterred in developed environments. Occasionally, in pursuit of prey, they fly into office building windowpanes, and so you may find one injured in an unexpected place one day. Holding one incorrectly will cause the bird undue stress, but if you've learned how to handle one properly, you may be able to save its life.

DATA

Length: 7.9–11.9 in.
Nocturnal.
They live hidden in the darkness. If you find one in town, take it to a vet or rescue center.

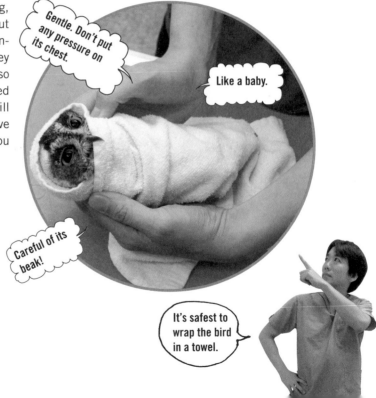

First, calm it down.

Being touched by humans causes a great deal of stress to wild animals. In some circumstances the shock can be so great that it kills them. The best method for making an owl feel at ease is to pick it up in a towel from behind, exerting light pressure at the back of the neck and on the legs. Then wrap the towel around it, as if it were a baby. When the bird is relaxed, the towel can be loosened, and parts of the body checked as necessary.

How to hold

Hold firmly, supporting the neck from behind.

When the towel is removed for treatment at the clinic, the legs are held firmly.

PRAIRIE DOGS

Lovable escape artists.

Prairie dogs can be naughty and difficult to handle. Despite their wild ways and the fact that they are generally less cooperative than a cat or a ferret, their behavior is often charming, and they grow fond of their owners. People like the contrasts in their character, hence their popularity as pets in Japan.

Large numbers were imported and sold as pets in the past, and now the market is supplied with domestically bred animals. With plenty around, don't be surprised if a neighbor's prairie dog finds its way into your house. If you don't catch it quickly, it may make a real mess. So it's a good idea to learn how to pick up and hold them.

DATA

Length: 13.7–17.7 in.
Character:
Soon acclimates to people. Normally lives in a group, so when it has contact with you it treats you as one of the gang.

Hold firmly.

Support its bottom with one hand. If its starts to wriggle, tighten your grip.

Constant vigilance!

First, close all doors in case it runs off. The fingers of one hand should go around the back of its neck and under its armpits. The other hand should keep a firm hold of one of its upper thighs. Do not relax your grip. Always be on your guard. If it starts to squirm loose, you can easily lose your grip. In case your hand slips, have a towel on the table beneath. If you think you can't control it with your hands, quickly wrap it up in a towel.

By wrapping a towel around the animal with only its head showing, the vet can check its eyes and the inside of its mouth.

HEDGEHOGS

Don't forget your leather gloves!

Popular in children's books and always a hit at the zoo . . . now certain types of hedgehogs have achieved additional fame as invasive species! Yes, they can now be found in the wild in parts of central Japan. On the bright side, your chances of coming across a hedgehog have dramatically increased. So how should you deal with one if you do?

DATA

Length: 6–10in.
Character:
Very shy, but once they're used to you, they'll look straight at you with their lovely eyes. Their favorite food: bugs.

When moving them, I always use leather gloves. It's not impossible to do it with bare hands, but you must be able to tolerate the pain and not drop them. I pick them up by the back and turn them over so that they are belly up on my palm. If a hedgehog is surprised or on the defensive, its spines will stick up on its back.

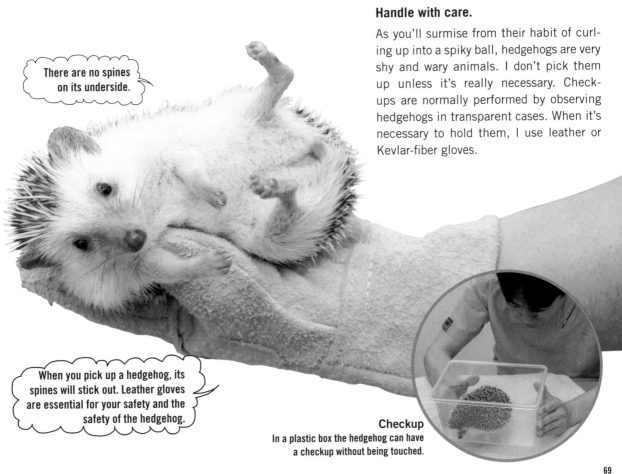

Handle with care.

As you'll surmise from their habit of curling up into a spiky ball, hedgehogs are very shy and wary animals. I don't pick them up unless it's really necessary. Check-ups are normally performed by observing hedgehogs in transparent cases. When it's necessary to hold them, I use leather or Kevlar-fiber gloves.

There are no spines on its underside.

When you pick up a hedgehog, its spines will stick out. Leather gloves are essential for your safety and the safety of the hedgehog.

Checkup
In a plastic box the hedgehog can have a checkup without being touched.

A WORD FROM THE EXPERT

Trimming claws.

One unexpectedly difficult thing about keeping animals is claw and nail trimming. If the owner tries to do it at home, the pet soon realizes that something unpleasant is going to happen and does its best to avoid it. Because of the tricky nature of this task, many owners don't do a very good job. That's where vets come in. We think carefully about how to trim claws.

Rabbit: Basic trim.

It's safest if there are two of you—one person holding the rabbit and the other trimming the claws. The rabbit should be held securely with its stomach facing the person trimming.

A one-person trim.

The rabbit should be held in the same way as when there are two people. This method is okay if the animal is docile.

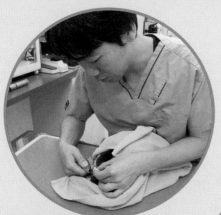

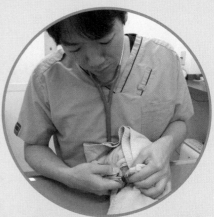

For unruly rabbits.

If the rabbit feels uncomfortable and is acting up, we wrap it in a towel so that only the feet show. Wrap the head and bottom firmly so that it can't get away.

Ferrets.

Cut the claws carefully while holding the ferret by the back of its neck. Holding them like this keeps them calm.

Prairie dogs.

Prairie dogs will do all they can to make this impossible, so they should be wrapped firmly in a towel with only their feet showing. This way you can control them and you won't be bitten.

Sugar gliders.

We hold the animal from behind in a laundry net so that the claws come through the holes. We cut the claws from the outside of the net. This method is also suitable for squirrels.

Tortoises and Turtles.

One person holds the animal with its legs showing while another cuts. Tortoise and turtle claws can get surprisingly long.

Hedgehogs.

You can't clip while holding hedgehogs, so we put them on firm wire mesh and cut the claws on their feet from underneath. They sometimes don't notice.

My Specialty: Hold Spirit

Normally, basic holding techniques are enough, but sometimes animals require special control for treatment. We have to consider size, delicacy of bones, state of health, etc.

Cats

Hold its four legs firmly, with one arm holding down its neck and head and the other its thighs. Adjust the pressure depending on how unruly the cat is.

Dogs

Put your arm around the dog's lower back and use your body weight to press down on the animal. Keep control of its front paws and head. If it still acts up, pull its front legs forward so that its tummy is flat against the floor or other surface. This will make it difficult for the dog to move. Injections are possible even for the most unwilling dogs held in this way.

Reptile Shop Owner Kazuhisa Yamada Holds Them Like This!

Most reptiles are wild and don't develop attachment to humans. But I'm selling them to be kept as pets, so of course I have to handle them. The first thing is to know about the species. Then I take stock of the conditions of the particular animal in front of me. I don't want to injure it—and I don't want to get injured myself.

PROFILE

Kazuhisa Yamada

Reptile shop owner. Takes pride in handling large and dangerous reptiles and amphibians. The store's motto is "If we sell it, we can hold it."

REPTILES

MONITOR LIZARDS

Don't drop your guard.

Monitor lizards can grow to be over six feet long. A dream animal for some kids! Their bodies are strong and their movements vigorous. They swish their tails when angry and sometimes jump at you. They're dangerous!

Their mouths are what you should really watch out for. A monitor lizard isn't poisonous, but its mouth is full of bacteria, and its sharp teeth tear things to shreds.

Next are the claws. A monitor lizard is a big, tree-climbing animal, so you can imagine how sharp and powerful its claws are. They can tear your flesh.

Finally, keep an eye on its long, whiplike tail. If that catches you, you'll have a welt on your skin.

Obviously, if you don't do things properly, you'll have real problems. So make sure you learn how to hold them!

DATA

Length: 4.5–8.2 ft.
Where?
Rivers and lakes in Southeast Asia.
Eats mammals, birds, fish, prawns, and crabs.
Gets used to people easily.
Sometimes females reproduce through parthenogenesis.

Asian Water Monitor

The tail moves like a whip. Be careful!

A lot of sharp teeth. A bite is very dangerous.

The claws are sharp and can gouge into your flesh. Be careful!

Approach Procedure: Monitor Lizards

1 Hold your hands out straight above the animal, and bring them down at the same time.

2 Take a firm grip.

3 Press down and keep the animal still.

4 Lift, keeping the tail under your arm.

Rock Monitor

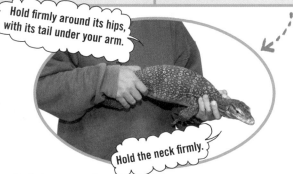

Hold firmly around its hips, with its tail under your arm.

Hold the neck firmly.

A docile specimen.

Be careful: Even a docile specimen may turn on you! Always hold the neck and front legs with one hand and the back legs and tail with the other. If it's held in this way, you can control it quickly. Be especially careful to keep a firm grip on the neck in case it tries to bite.

A vicious specimen.

If you're dealing with a vicious specimen, it's critical to keep a very firm hold. Grip the neck and front legs with one hand and the back legs and tail with the other. Keep the tail firmly under your arm so that it can't hurt you. If you loosen your grip for a moment, you'll almost definitely be injured.

MEDIUM-SIZED LIZARDS

Smaller than monitors, but don't let that fool you.

If you can hold a monitor lizard, don't assume that holding a medium-sized one will be a piece of cake. It's a different type of challenge, so stay alert. It may be smaller, but its jaws are still powerful and its teeth are very sharp, so holding one is still risky business. Those teeth can tear at your flesh.

These lizards have a lot of stamina.

A temperamental midsize lizard is extremely hard to hold. You don't have to worry too much about the claws, but it will try to bite. And it won't give up easily. It's got a lot of stamina and will carry on struggling. Keep a firm hold on the neck and the root of the tail and don't relax your grip.

DATA

Length: 15.7–19.7 in.
Where?
Africa, in dry savannah and rocky places.
Eats crickets and other insects. In the wild, sometimes lives on anthills. Can cope with changes in humidity and temperature. Gets used to humans and is easy to keep.

Sudan Plated Lizard

The teeth will drill into your flesh if you're not careful.

How to hold

Medium-sized iguana.

Hold one of these in the same way as a Sudan plated lizard. The important point with an iguana is to be as careful of its claws as of its mouth. It's a gracious loser, and as long as you hold it firmly, it will stop misbehaving, so you don't have to hold it too tight. But without experience, it would probably be a mistake to loosen your grip once you're holding it.

DATA

Length: 3.2–3.9 ft.
Where?
Cuba—sunny places. An herbivore, eating plants and fruit. It gets used to people easily. A highly endangered species and strictly protected. Widely bred outside Cuba.

Cuban Rock Iguana

COMMON LEOPARD GECKOS

The thumb is key.

Lizards—particularly frilled-neck lizards—have had their share of press in the past, but it's hard to imagine any other member of the lizard family closer to our hearts than the common leopard gecko.

In Japan, celebrities have them, children have them—people of all sorts love their common leopard geckos. Go on a train or into a café, and the chances are you'll overhear a girl chatting about hers. At the airport you may hear a little boy asking if his can go in his carry-on baggage. It's a strange world for the over thirties!

Well, reptile fans, here's how to hold this lovely creature. Make sure you master both the approach and the subsequent handling.

DATA

Length: 7.8–11.8 in.
Where?
Desert and dry wilderness in the Middle East. Almost all common leopard geckos that you see in Japan are bred in captivity. There's very little trade in wild ones. Breeding is simple, and they eat bugs and processed reptile feed.

Approach Procedure: Leopard Geckos

1 Move your hands towards it from both sides.

2 Push it up onto your hand.

3 That's it.

How to hold

Always be gentle.

The common leopard gecko is actually pretty difficult to hold. If you try to control it by holding tight, its tail may come off, or you may get bitten. So just get it onto your hand and lay your thumb lightly on its back.

TOKAY GECKOS

Dangerous characters.

Have a finger on each side of its jaws.

Southeast Asia. A lodge in the dead of night. A strange cry shatters the silence. Fighting my fear I switch on the light and to my horror find a huge, brightly colored gecko on the wall above the bed. My wife is frozen in terror. My children are screaming. What shall I do? It was supposed to be nice, this place . . . cost quite a bit . . .

Well, get ready. Now's your chance to learn how to pick up a tokay gecko!

Approach Procedure: Tokays

1 Its standard reaction is anger.

2 When you see your chance, bring your hand down swiftly onto the gecko so that it can't move.

3 Adjust your hold.

4 Lift it up.

How to hold

Bitten!

It's win or lose.

The tokay is a large and vicious gecko. I've seen quite a few, but none of them has been unassuming. All of them open their mouths wide and give a loud, threatening cry. As a gecko, the tokay has a tail that can come off. But it's a win-or-lose situation, so pin the gecko's body down quickly with your palm, and position one finger on each side of its jaws. Unless you try to grab the tail itself, it probably won't come off.

85

MEDIUM-SIZED NONVENOMOUS SNAKES

Most bite . . . and probably will! But they're not poisonous.

People who don't like snakes tend to find them—that's because they're looking out for them. It's part of a human's wonderful built-in security system. If you see one in time, it's easily avoided. But what if you suddenly step on one? Or what if there's one up a tree that you have to walk under? Wouldn't you feel safer if you knew how to handle it?

Approach Procedure: Green Tree Python

Go for the head.

Grip firmly between thumb and forefinger.

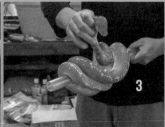

Pull sharply away.

Hold the head like this.

Green Tree Python

Bloodshed inevitable.

Given the chance, green tree pythons and other tree-living boas and pythons will almost always bite. They're not poisonous, but their teeth are long, so if you're bitten, there'll be a fair amount of blood. As a reptile dealer, I don't want that to happen in front of a customer, so I have to control the snake's head. I use a three-point hold, with my thumb and middle finger on either side of its mouth and my forefinger on the top of its head. If I then wrap the snake just a little around my arm, it will relax. When releasing the snake, I start by removing the tail from my arm. The head should be released last.

DATA

Length: 3.9–5.9 ft.
Where?
Rain forests of Indonesia and New Guinea.
They spend most of the day curled up in trees. They eat mammals and birds. Many are nervous and will bite humans. Tree snakes have longer fangs than ground snakes, so their bites are more painful.

Known locally as "Akamata" and certain to bite.

There are a lot of TV programs in Japan featuring dopey comedians getting into a fuss about being bitten. Often, the snake involved is a Ryukyu odd-tooth. It's a tough customer, who's guaranteed to attempt to bite you. Hold it by the head with one hand and support the body with the other, about halfway along.

Ryukyu Odd-Tooth Snake

DATA

Length: 3–4.5 ft.
Where?
Forests and fields, etc. All over the Okinawa and Amami islands. Eats bugs, mammals, and birds as well as their carcasses and eggs. Excitable. Always tries to bite when held.

1
An Akamata ready to attack.

Approach Procedure: Akamata

2
Here I got my timing wrong and was bitten.

3
Got the timing right this time.

4
Bring your hand down decisively on its head.

5
Take a firm grip on both sides of the mouth.

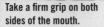

A bite—but not much of one.

A colubrid less likely to bite.

Hold the milk snake gently about halfway along its body and wrap its tail around your arm. Allow its head and front half of its body to move freely, and control its basic direction. But if you try to grab or interfere with the head, you may get bitten. So watch out!

DATA

Length: 1.6–6.2 ft.
Where?
Forests in North, Central, and South America.
Color and patterning mimic the highly venomous coral snake. Have long been kept as pets in the US and are widely bred.

Milk Snake

SLOWWORMS

A snakelike lizard—it'll spin to get away!

Handsome, imposing—but legless. What is this? A snake? A supernatural being? If you suddenly encountered a creature like this, you'd certainly want to know its identity! This bizarre individual is more difficult to hold than either a snake or a normal lizard—it takes nerve, but it has to be done. You can't grab the tops of its legs—it hasn't got any—unlike a normal lizard. And unlike a snake, it can't be wrapped around your arm—its body's not flexible enough. What can you do? Here's the solution.

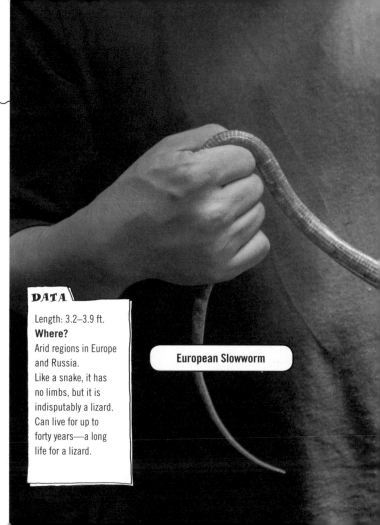

European Slowworm

DATA

Length: 3.2–3.9 ft.
Where?
Arid regions in Europe and Russia.
Like a snake, it has no limbs, but it is indisputably a lizard. Can live for up to forty years—a long life for a lizard.

Breathtakingly handsome.

Be cautious.

The right amount of pressure.

Put one hand around the neck, so that it can't bite, and the other about where the back legs might be if it had any. Slowworms can be tough to hold and may resist by spinning around like a drill. If it starts doing that, make sure you keep your hand in the same position around its neck, but allow it to spin freely. It won't give up easily, but if you give up first, you'll have lost.

91

SNAKE-NECKED TURTLES

They can bite in all directions.

Most ordinary folk find this creature, with its extraordinarily long neck, very odd. But for turtle maniacs, it's hugely popular and very valuable. Some types can set you back several thousand dollars. Intrigued? Well, this top-shelf turtle is tough to control and bites a lot. If you find one, how do you pick it up?

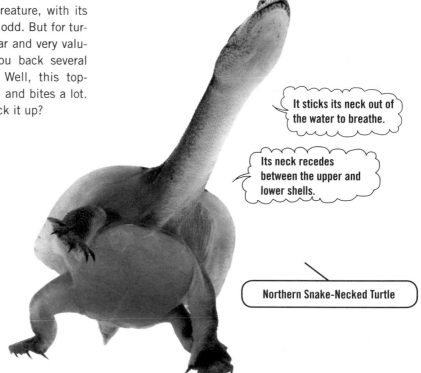

> It sticks its neck out of the water to breathe.

> Its neck recedes between the upper and lower shells.

Northern Snake-Necked Turtle

DATA
Length: 9.8–137 in.
Where?
Rivers and swamps in Indonesia, New Guinea, and Australia. A great swimmer, it eats fish, prawns, and crabs. Unlike native Japanese turtles, it cannot hide its neck and head completely under its shell—it's a type of side-necked turtle (Pleurodira) that lives only in the Oceanian region.

Its shell is covered in scales.

Hold the tops of its back legs.

How to hold

The key point: get your thumb firmly against one of its back legs and hold the lower shell tight.

Where do your hands go?

For most turtles you simply have to hold the sides of the top shell. But for the snake-necked turtle, that won't work. You'll just be bitten. With a neck that long, it can come at you from every angle. Holding the back of the top shell is an option, but they have a powerful kick and long claws, which can be pretty painful. So if that fails, the best thing is to control the lower shell with one hand and have the other hand firmly around the turtle's neck.

93

SOFTSHELL TURTLES

Hold tight!

"If it bites, it won't let go till it hears a clap of thunder." So goes the old saying about the softshell. It's quick and has a long neck—and if it's upset, it will bite. Its jaws are powerful and if you get bitten, you'll be badly injured. If you pick one up, be sure to do so in a way that prevents it from biting you. If it does bite and you keep it up in the air, then it'll hang on for a long time. But you won't have to wait for thunder. Lower it on the ground or in water and it'll let go.

DATA

Length: 20–31.5 in.
Where?
Northern and central Africa; the Arabian Peninsula. Rivers, ponds, marshlands, and lakes. Occasionally the sea. Larger types have particularly large females. Eat fish, shrimp, and crabs.

The undershell is also called the "plastron."

Grip the rear of the shell firmly.

African Softshell Turtle

Don't be bitten!

Softshells are popular as pets these days and they're pricey, so we're very careful handling them. The last thing we want is to get bitten in the shop and find ourselves dropping it, or banging it against the floor in front of a customer. Normally people hold the back of the shell tight in both hands. Even then the terrapin can cause problems if it gets upset. To be really safe, hold the undershell with your fingers and thumbs firmly under the tops of its back legs.

Even small ones have a very nasty bite!

The most dangerous field trip.

Now that you've learned how to pick up and hold so many reptiles, you probably want to test your skills.

I don't think there are any animals that can't be held using the techniques in this book. But there are some you should never try to hold: poisonous snakes, constrictors, and crocodiles. You're not going to come across one of these in the street, but I'm saying this just in case.

I visited Izu Shaboten Zoo on the Izu peninsula where I got special permission to handle some dangerous creatures. I had help from Tsuyoshi Shirawa, the head of the zoo, who has probably handled more dangerous creatures than anybody else in Japan.

A LARGE BUT AGILE
SOFTSHELL.

Not all terrapins are small. The bigger they are, the more powerful their bite—and they're very agile in the water, so they can be really dangerous. You have to avoid being bitten at all costs—a bite could break bones. So you get behind it, grab the back legs firmly, and lift it up. Make sure it doesn't bite your legs.

ALLIGATOR SNAPPING TURTLE.

At one time the alligator snapping turtle was a hot topic. Their amazing appearance enticed animal collectors. But a number have escaped or been set free by owners who couldn't cope with looking after them. They're fierce and will snap at anything they see moving in front of them. So when picking one up, you have to approach from behind. You take a firm grip on the front of the upper shell above the neck with one hand and on the rear of the upper shell with the other. Then you lift it up, with the animal in front of you and facing forward. Held like that, it won't be able to bite you however hard it tries.

TO BE AVOIDED, EVEN BY COMMITTED MASOCHISTS.

Nobody can deal with a giant snake alone. Even if it's not hungry, it may coil itself around you in a way that makes it very difficult to escape if there's no one around to help. They squeeze their prey to death before swallowing it, so the more you squirm, the more they'll squeeze. However much of a masochist you may be, don't let yourself be alone with one of these. It's dangerous. Make sure you have at least two people around. One should hold the tail firmly; the other should hold the head and control its movement. It's best to keep the head under control so that you don't get bitten. If the snake is a bit smaller, one person may be able to hold it on their own, but somebody else should always be present. And if there are two people, one of them can try wrapping the snake around his neck, if you like that sort of thing.

Golden Boa Constrictor

ALWAYS EXPECT IT TO BITE!

If you're bitten by an anaconda and you try to pull away quickly, you'll rip your flesh. It will be agony. And an anaconda will always bite, so you have to have a very firm grip on its neck straightaway. Of course, it's got to breathe, so not too tight. Anacondas are slippery, so leather gloves help, and they offer some protection if you're bitten.

Like a scarf?

Anaconda

POISONOUS SNAKES—
USE A THREE-POINT HOLD.

There are many types of poisonous snake, but this basic method can be applied to all. With your thumb and middle finger, grip it securely just behind its jaws. This stops its neck from moving. Your index finger should be on the back of its head. With this three-point hold, it won't be able to bite. If you keep it steady with its body or tail wrapped on a snake hook, it won't get too upset.

Snake hook

Approach Procedure

1

Pin the head down with a snake hook.

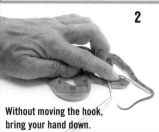

2

Without moving the hook, bring your hand down.

3

Take a three-point hold.

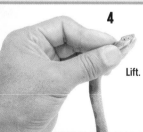

4

Lift.

The ringhals spits poison through the air, so face protection should be worn.

Rattlesnakes make a frightening noise, but the way of holding them is the same.

POISONOUS LIZARDS
ARE RATHER EXCITABLE.

It's not only snakes that are poisonous! There are poisonous lizards too! As with other lizards, you hold them by their head and the root of their tail. If their bodies have warmed in the sun, they tend to be very aggressive, so keepers wear a leather glove on the hand they use to hold the head.

CROCODILES
ARE REALLY STRONG.

If they're small, you can handle them like a lizard—with one hand on the neck and one at the root of the tail. But dealing with a big one is a different matter. Keeping an eye on its powerful tail, step onto the crocodile's mouth and put a thick rubber band around its jaws so that it can't open them. Its jaws have tremendous force when shutting, but not so much when opening, so a strong band around its mouth will stop it from biting. Then, still wary of its tail, two people pick it up. The key is not to loosen your grip or let your guard down. In any case, it's better to leave picking up big crocs to others.

Approach Procedure: Crocodiles

1 First put a noose around its neck.

2 Drag the crocodile out.

3 Put your foot on its head so that it can't bite.

4 Put a thick rubber band around its mouth.

5 Now you can feel safer.

6 When the crocodile has quieted down . . .

7 Two people heave it up.

AFTERWORD

I've loved creatures of all kinds since I was a child. I used to catch them and look after them. I got bitten and stung and sometimes badly injured. Occasionally, because of my ignorance, an animal died.

People who as children have that kind of interest in and experience with animals often remain attuned to the natural world as adults.

That's what I'm like.

Nowadays education relating to wildlife and nature emphasizes conservation and protection. In that context, catching animals and keeping them tends to be frowned upon.

Children are sometimes told off if they catch living things. If they're on private property or within a protected area, then that is called for. But the same can happen if a child brings a creature home from a local stream, for example.

If they're told they're not allowed to catch living things, their interest goes elsewhere. As a result, ignorance about nature grows.

Children's minds aren't stimulated by bossy adults. They learn by trial and error which leads to real understanding.

To me, merely watching animals is the same as not being interested in them. Instead of talking loftily about animal protection, I'd rather pick an animal up, show it to children, and give them some practical advice:

"Hold them like this."

"If you hold it like that, the animal won't be comfortable."

"You'll catch your finger if you hold it like that. It'll hurt."

"You could take this home and look after it. It would be interesting."

"If it's difficult to look after, let it go."

I like to encourage them to get outside, come into contact with animals, and spend time with them. "Go camping, have a barbecue, and if you make a mess, clean it up before you go home!"

I really hope more adults in the future will encourage children's interest in wildlife and the creatures around us. I think knowing how to pick up and hold animals is one way of being inspiring as an adult.

So pick up an animal safely and carefully and open the minds of others.

—Toshimitsu Matsuhashi, animal photographer

AN INDEX OF CREATURES APPEARING IN THIS BOOK

35 cockroach, Madagascar Hissing *Gromphadorhina portentosa*

35 cockroach, Yaeyama-madara *Rhabdoblatta yayeyamana*

12 crab, Benitsuke *Thalamita pelsarti*

13 crab, Blue Land *Cardisoma hirtipes*

12 crab, Coconut *Birgus latro*

13 crab, Japanese Freshwater *Geothelphusa dehaani*

11 crayfish, Japanese *Cambaroides japonicus*

10 crayfish, Red Swamp *Procambarus clarkii*

3 cricket, Eastern Bush *Gampsocleis mikado*

4 cricket, Emma Field *Teleogryllus emma*

4 cricket, *Kubikirigisu* Bush *Euconocephalus thunbergi*

7 damselfly, Mortonagrion *Mortonagrion selenion*

55 dog, Miniature Dachshund *Canis lupus familiaris*

54 dog, Great Pyrenees *Canis lupus familiaris*

55 dog, Shiba Inu *Canis lupus familiaris*

6 dragonfly, Black-Striped Lesser Emperor *Anax parthenope julius*

7 dragonfly, Globe Skimmer *Pantala flavescens*

7 dragonfly, Golden-Ringed *Anotogaster sieboldii*

6 dragonfly, Harabiro *Lyriothemis pachygastra*

7 dragonfly, Konoshime *Sympetrum baccha matutinum*

58–59 Ferret *Mustela putorius furo*

17 frog, Japanese Tree *Hyla japonica*

WHERE THE EXPERTS WORK: SHOPS, ANIMAL HOSPITALS, ZOOS

Takahiro Goto's shop
Keiyodo
3-9-7 Mukaihara, Midori-ku, Sagamihara City, Kanazawa
Prefecture 252-0104
Tel: 042-783-1081

Kenichi Tamukai's animal hospital
Denen Chofu Animal Hospital
2-1-3 Denen Chofu. Ota-ku, Tokyo 145-0071
Tel: 03-5483-7676 Fax: 03-5483-7656
Closed on Thursdays
http://www5f.biglobe.ne.jp/~dec-ah/

Kazuhisa Yamada's shop
Toko Campur
1F Aoki Coopo, 1-20-13 Asahi-cho, Atsugi City, Kanagawa
Prefecture 243-0014
Tel and Fax: 046-227-2233
Closed on Mondays
http://www.asiajp.net

With thanks for special cooperation
Watch! Touch! Amazing!!
Sensory Zoo
iZoo
Japan's largest amphibian and reptile zoo. A sensory zoo that gives
visitors experiences they've never had anywhere before.
406-2 Kawazu-cho, Kamo-gun, Shizuoka Prefecture 413-0513
Tel: 0558-34-0003
http://www.izoo.co.jp/

About the Author

Toshimitsu Matsuhashi

After working for many years at an aquarium, Toshimitsu decided to become an animal photographer. He produces children's books using his photos of wildlife.

He also runs animal-holding workshops to give children opportunities for coming into contact with animals.

http://www.matsu8.com

Additional photographs supplied by Kaito Shimizu, Kenji Tamura, Shinta Kano, Itsumi Kano, Naoto Tokozumi, Hidemi Matsunae, Riona Hayakawa, Yui Shimizu.